Northumbria:
kingdom by the sea

Daniel Bell

Northumbria:
kingdom by the sea

Photographs by David Bell
Text by Michael W. Marshall

Keepdate Publishing

Published by Keepdate Publishing Ltd
21 Portland Terrace
Newcastle upon Tyne NE2 1QQ
UK

© Photographs by David Bell & text by Michael W. Marshall 1996

First Edition 1996

ISBN 1-899506-05-5

Apart from any fair dealing for the purposes of research or private study, or criticism or review as permitted under the Copyright, Designs and Patents Act 1988, this publication may not be reproduced, stored or transmitted, in any form or by any means, without the prior permission in writing of the publishers, or in the case of reprographic reproductions in accordance with the terms of licences issued by the Copyright Licensing Agency. Inquiries concerning reproduction outside those terms should be sent to the publishers at the address above.

Designed and typeset by Keepdate Publishing Ltd, Newcastle upon Tyne.
Printed in Hong Kong.

Contents

Introduction: the Tweed to the Tees 1

Berwick to Bamburgh 5

Seahouses to Warkworth 25

Amble to Blyth 49

Seaton Sluice to Whitley Bay 69

The Mouth of the Tyne 77

From Wear to Tees 91

Introduction:
the Tweed to the Tees

Northumbria is a magical, deeply historical land. It is an ancient kingdom and diverse images cut through its long history: quiet monastic life; gentle scholarship; Celtic art; magnificent illuminated manuscripts; St Aidan; the Venerable Bede; Caedmon, the visionary poet; the savage rape of village and religious settlement by Viking, Scot, Gael and Angle. The centre of European civilisation in the seventh and eighth centuries, it led the world almost a thousand years later in the Industrial Revolution.

Much of Northumbria's history took place along its coasts. The Angles and Vikings landed their longships on its beaches. Great castles, some darkly ruined and austere, others perfectly restored and of almost fairy tale appearance dominate many of the coastal headlands and tell of Northumbria's violent wars with Scotland. Its deeply religious, cultural and more peaceful history is reflected in the magnificent and elegant monastic remains that reach skyward from island and sea cliff and chronicle Britain's early Christianity. The pit heads and slag heaps of its seaside collieries signal the presence of one of Britain's richest coal seams – now no longer being worked.

Today the scenery of coastal Northumbria, stretching between the Tweed and the Tees, is rich, varied and some of the most spectacular in Britain: long, lonely beaches bordered by rolling sand dunes; majestic sea cliffs unchanged since the Angles and Saxons; idyllic fishing villages; picturesque offshore islands; urban sprawl and land scarred by nineteenth and twentieth century industrial pollution.

Northumbria was an Anglian kingdom. It was violently formed from the conflicts that followed the collapse of Roman Britain. A slow collapse that began in 410 when Honorius the Roman emperor, threatened by the break down of the Rhine frontier in 406, told the Britons that he was unable to supply any troops and that the island had to fend for itself. Many legionnaires had already departed to defend the Roman Empire and to fight on the Rhine front leaving behind peaceful, unprotected Romano-British settlements that were easy prey to marauding Irish, Scottish and German tribes. The fierce German tribes sailed in from the North Sea to plunder the North East coast, the tough Gaelic speaking Irish crossed the Irish Sea to attack the west coast villages and the unconquered Picts and Scots swept down from the North through the largely defunct Hadrian's Wall – long, but no longer the sign of Roman stability and the frontier of Roman Britain for some 250 years.

Throughout the whole of the fifth century tribes from lower Germany – Angles, Saxons and Jutes, continued to invade and settle along the East and North East coast of Britain to create Angleland or England and push the Celtic British westwards. By the end of the sixth century there were two Anglian kingdoms in the North beyond the Humber – Bernicia and Deira.

In 547 a warrior band of Angles, led by Ida the Flame Bearer, sailed from Yorkshire to land on a wide sweep of sandy beach some 50 miles north of the River Tyne. There the Angles built a stronghold on a basalt platform where Bamburgh Castle is today and perhaps the same site of the coastal hill fort of 'Din Guayroi' that was built earlier by the Britons of Brynaich. The Anglo-Saxon Chronicle: *In this year (547) Ida assumed the kingdom, for whom arose the royal race of the Northanhymbra, and reigned twelve years, and he built Bebbanburh, which was first enclosed by a hedge, (stockade) and afterwards by a wall (rampart)*. The Angles might have attacked the Britons of Strathclyde and for a period things went badly for the Angles as they were forced back to their coastal forts at Bamburgh and perhaps Holy Island only to be saved by the outbreak of dissension among the Britons.

In the south of the region, settlements along the rivers of the Humber estuary and more generally the East Riding of Yorkshire, was the kingdom of Deira: its centre became the city of York. Deira was probably an older but smaller kingdom than Bernicia. Traditionally, the royal dynasties of Bernicia and Deira were of similar ancestry, each claiming direct descent from the god Woden. According to legend, King Aethelric of Bernicia acquired the kingdom of Deira from King Aelle, the first recorded King of Deira, on Aelle's death-bed. Aethelric's son, Aethelfrith, married Aelle's daughter and reigned over the two kingdoms, which became collectively known as *Northanhymbra*. Aethelfrith 'the Twister' succeeded to the kingdom of *Northanhymbra* or 'Northumbria' in 593. He was a powerful warrior and expanded Bernicia westwards through the Tyne valley and there is evidence from place names that his kingdom stretched from the Solway to the Mersey. At its peak the kingdom of Northumbria embraced much of the land between the Humber and the Forth.

During the seventh and eighth centuries Christian monasteries and culture flourished in the kingdom of Northumbria. The Celts re-exerted their influence when the Celtic missionary St Aidan established the Lindisfarne monastery on Holy Island. Many other fine monasteries were built at Tynemouth, Jarrow, Wearmouth, Hartlepool and Whitby. Scholarship flourished. The Venerable

Bede, who lived in the Jarrow monastery from 682, produced his famous *Ecclesiastical History of the English People*, a priceless Anglo-Saxon history.

But peace was short lived. In 787 the first Viking longships landed on Northumbria's coasts and the kingdom began its slow decline. The Vikings entered the Tyne and, seven years later, they returned to sack and loot the Jarrow monastery. The Vikings returned again in 875 and this time in earnest. Their leader Halfdan sailed a fleet of longships in to the Tyne estuary and attacked and looted Tynemouth monastery. Halfdan spent the winter on an island not far from the mouth of the river and in the following spring laid waste to much of Northumbria. Lindisfarne and Hexham monasteries were burnt and the monks that did not flee were massacred. By the end of the ninth century the kingdom was in serious trouble, threatened on three fronts by Saxons, Vikings and Scots.

The new Scottish kingdom formed when the Picts and Scots united in 844 and became a formidable and long-lasting threat to Northumbria. By the 960s the Scots had pushed down almost to the Tyne destroying much of Northumbria which soon declined from a kingdom to an earldom. The defeated, pious Anglo-Saxon kings and notables of Northumbria gradually gave all their land between the Tyne and the Tees to the bishop and church of Durham. Following the Norman conquest, Northumbria was further weakened when the earldom lost church and lands to the powerful bishop of Durham cathedral and castle.

Today 'Northumbria' is a loosely defined region usually considered to be bordered by the River Tweed in the north and the River Tees in the south and includes the counties of Northumberland, Durham, Tyne and Wear as well as the industrialised area north of the Tees. Four rivers flow through the region: the Tweed, the Tyne, the Wear and the Tees and all have played important roles in the history of the North East. The Tweed, a border river much fought over in the Middle Ages by Scottish and English knights; the rivers Tyne and Wear, both of which played and continue to play a major role in the industrial and economic development of Britain and the North East, as does the Tees and its much industrialised banks. For hundreds of years the Tees was a Yorkshire frontier defining the point at which the power of the king of England declined and the Bishop of Durham's began.

Berwick to Bamburgh

After centuries of dispute the Scottish border is finally considered to lie four miles north of Berwick-upon-Tweed, reaching the Northumbrian coast at a small, rock-faced bay – Marshall Meadows. The 150 ft high, dark Carboniferous rock cliffs soon disappear into the flat table rock of the coast that leads to the town of Berwick-upon-Tweed. Berwick-upon-Tweed is Northumbria's and England's most northern town and sits on a peninsular between the sea and the River Tweed. It became Scottish in 1018 when the Scots succeeded in creating the Tweed as the frontier between Scotland and Northumbria. During the Middle Ages the town changed hands some thirteen times before it finally became English in 1482.

The River Tweed is one of the world's most famous salmon rivers where a week's fishing with rod, line and fly can cost as much as £5,000. Near its mouth the river is spanned by three bridges: nearest to the sea is a pretty, pink-stoned 15 arch bridge built between 1611 and 1635 and still carrying traffic across to the small town of Tweedmouth which is situated on the south side of the river; next inland is the functional, concrete Royal Tweed bridge that was built to carry the ever increasing A1 motor traffic; furthest away from the sea is the gracefully arched Royal Border Bridge, a railway bridge that was built in 1847 by Robert Stephenson to carry the steam trains of the London-Edinburgh railway. It was opened in 1850 by Queen Victoria and Prince Albert and is still in use.

Berwick is a fortified town and its unusual, low-walled, earth-topped Elizabethan fortifications were built in the sixteenth century as a means of defending the town against the heavy cannons that were then easily breaching the walls of more traditionally constructed high-walled castles. Another novelty in the town is a spireless and towerless parish church, Holy Trinity, that was built between 1648 and 1652 during the Puritanical days of Cromwell's Commonwealth when no doubt those features were considered to be frivolous.

Across on the south bank of the River the towns of Tweedmouth and Spittal merge. Spittal is a small seaside town with a sandy beach that ends in a collection of rocks above which is the start of a coastal path that leads to Bamburgh castle and beyond, and passes along some of the most spectacular coastal scenery in Britain. The main London-Edinburgh railway line runs close to the sea south of Spittal and is crossed by a road that leads from the A1 to Seahouses at the head of Cocklawburn beach. The south part of this sandy bay is a nature reserve and here, in the spring, the dunes are a mass of wild flowers. There are sandstone outcrops along this part of the coast and at the tiny hamlet of Cheswick there are remains of several lime kilns. After Cheswick and towards Lindisfarne or Holy Island are miles of wonderful sandy beaches and grass covered dunes that in the right season are alive with birds and flowers. It is tempting but dangerous to walk across the sandy wastes of Goswick Sands to Holy Island as the rising tide runs fast.

A high point in all this flat coastal land is Beal, a collection of farm buildings on a small hill. The hill drops away to the causeway which is the relatively safe, metalled-road to Holy Island. The concrete blocks, World War II invasion defences which border the coastal path that leads to the south and north of the road, are in stark contrast to the crenelations and towers of romantic Lindisfarne Castle that so proudly dominates Holy Island. The castle was creatively restored by the architect Edwin Lutyens in 1902 from a ruined fort that was built in 1549 by Edward VI as a defence against the Scots.

The three mile causeway to Holy Island is uncovered for about three to four hours around each low tide. The exact crossing times are prominently displayed but still the occasional tourist's car is stopped by the fast, incoming tide and the refuge hut on the causeway fulfils its designated role. The old pilgrim crossing over the sand flats is still visible, marked by poles, and was perhaps the route taken by the Christian monk Aidan when he travelled from Iona at the request of Oswald, king of Northumbria, to found the Lindisfarne monastery on Holy Island.

The Vikings destroyed Aidan's monastery but fortunately not the wonderful seventh century *Lindisfarne Gospels* that were lovingly made there. They are still in existence in the British Museum – a tribute to the beauty of Celtic art and the patience, industry and care of the Northumbrian monks. The monastery and church remained derelict for some two hundred years. In 1093 a Norman priory was built on the island from red Goswick sandstone along similar lines to Durham Cathedral – the priory was intended to be a monastic branch of the cathedral. It became a ruin in the sixteenth century following the dissolution of the monasteries. Not far away is the well preserved twelfth/thirteenth century Parish church.

The lives of the small population of Holy Island are still governed by the tides. Men fish out of Holy Island's harbour for lobster and crab and they continue to use the transit beacons built in 1860 on Guile Point, the northern end of Ross Back Sands, to enter the harbour. On the harbour's foreshore are the upturned remains of the wooden herring fishing vessels, Scottish Fifies and Zulus that once sailed after the vast shoals of herring that migrated down the east coast of Britain. The herring have gone as has much of the in-shore fishing industry; the island and village are nowadays kept alive by the tourists who brave the causeway crossing.

Lindisfarne Nature Reserve, made up of Holy Island Sands and Fenham Flats, is the huge area of sand and salt marsh that lies between Holy Island and the shore. In winter the reserve is full of Brent geese who feed off the flats and sea grass until spring arrives. Another less extensive flat is Budle Bay to the south of Ross Back sands. A sandy ridge almost cuts off Budle Bay, also home to large numbers of waders and sea-birds, from the sea. Some two miles south is a famous Northumbrian stronghold that rises steeply out of the sand dunes: Bamburgh castle.

This is an ancient fort. The Romans used its natural defence site as did the Britons. The Angle king, Aethelfrith, grandson of Ida the Flame Bearer, renamed the castle after his wife Bebba. This became Bebba-burgh, Bebba's Town, and eventually the town and castle of Bamburgh. It was a Northumbrian king's castle until it was captured by Athelstan of Wessex, grandson of Alfred the Great. The Vikings destroyed much of the castle in 993; the Normans rebuilt; it decayed again and was largely and lavishly rebuilt by Lord Armstrong between 1894-1905. The pretty village of Bamburgh at the foot of the castle is much visited in summer by tourists and not without reason: there are attractive eighteenth century cottages; its church is near the site where St Aidan died; there is a museum dedicated to Grace Darling, daughter of the Longstone lighthouse keeper who in 1838 rescued nine men from the Forfarshire aground on an Inner Farne reef by rowing an open boat out to the ship with her father.

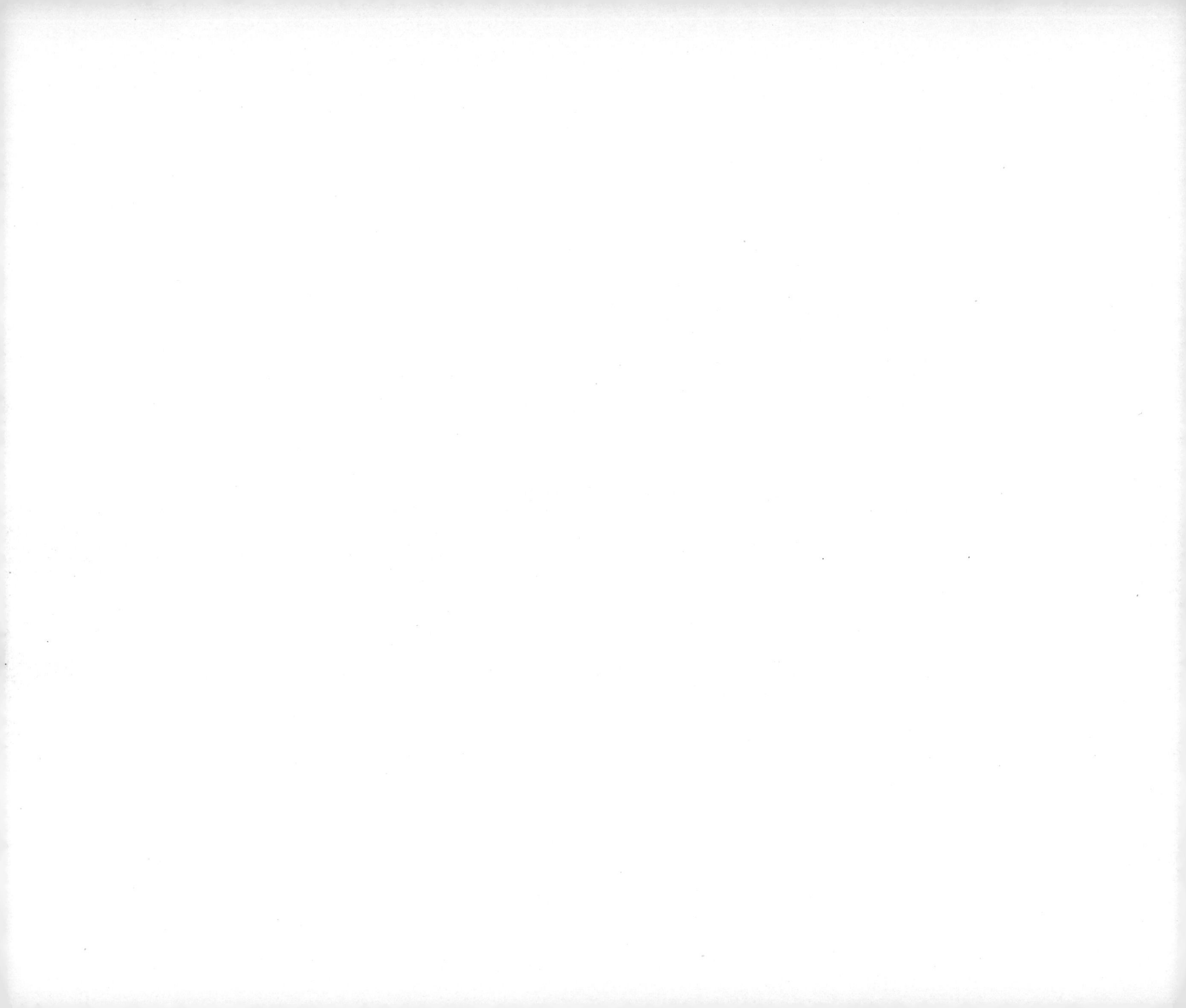

Berwick upon Tweed seen from Tweedmouth.

Berwick: 18th Century graves in Holy Trinity Church yard.

The golden sands of Cocklawburn Beach.

Fascinating rock stratification on Cocklawburn Beach.

Expanse of farmland between Cheswick and Cheswick Sands.

World War II invasion defences south of Beal Point.

The refuge from fast tides on the Causeway to Holy Island.

Holy Island: ruins of the Priory Church, built in the same period as Durham Cathedral.

Holy Island: the harbour and castle.

Holy Island: the characteristic fishermen's huts made from upturned herring boats.

Holy Island: the picturesque village seen from the castle.

Guile Point at the northern end of Ross Sands, one of two 100ft high navigation beacons built in 1860.

Budle Bay.

Bamburgh: the village dominated by the massive bulk of the castle.

Bamburgh beach, sea, sand, sun and solitude.

Seahouses to Warkworth

South of Bamburgh Castle, surrounded by large caravan parks and much visited by tourists, is Seahouses. It has a bustling fishing port with a fleet of cobles and trawlers and, in season, some of the cobles find it more profitable to act as ferry boats and offer day trips to visit the nesting birds on the Farne Islands. Farne is probably derived from a Celtic word 'ferran' or 'land'.

There are about 28 islands in the Farne Islands and the largest and the nearest, the Inner Farne, is about a mile and a half offshore. Some fifteen of the islands stay above high water, depending on the height of the tide, and thousands of sea birds, terns, kittiwakes, cormorants, puffins, eiders, fulmars and razorbills breed on the islands as well as – much to the dislike of the local fishermen – a large colony of grey seals.

Saint Aidan meditated on the Inner Farne (or Farne Island as it is sometimes called) and in 676 Saint Cuthbert, before becoming Prior of Lindisfarne monastery, lived a hermit's life there for eight years in a simple hut built of stone and turf. After two years as Prior of Lindisfarne he returned to the island and died there in 687. His body was taken to Durham cathedral during the Viking attacks on coastal Northumbria. A fourteenth century chapel on the island was named after him and in 1500 the Prior of Durham built a tower on Farne Island over the probable site of Saint Cuthbert's cell.

South of Seahouses is Beadnell, a small village that is remarkable for its well preserved eighteenth century lime kilns and delightful little harbour. The local fishermen store their creels and fishing gear in the arches of the kilns. The wide and sweeping sands of Beadnell Bay stretch to the south and west of the harbour before ending in the low rocks of Snook and Newton Points. Lower Newton-by-the-Sea nestles behind a superb rocky natural harbour which in fine weather is a delight for the audacious east coast yachtsperson but less well liked in a north east gale! Lower Newton's quaint green is surrounded on three sides by white-washed fishermen's cottages and at the top of the open square away from the bathing beach is a tiny pub.

Embleton village lies about a mile away from the dunes and beaches of Embleton Bay. It has a vicar's pele tower that was built in 1395 and it is still the home of the vicar whose church was built in 1320 on the site of a Norman church. There is invigorating golfing to be had on the links behind the dunes of Embleton Bay and the walker will find much solitude and tranquillity on this mile stretch of golden sand. Like Beadnell Bay the sands of Embleton Bay end in rocks and boulders but this time the rocks sit at the foot of sheer basalt sea cliffs that rise dramatically out of the sea. Sitting on the cliff are the brooding and stark ruins of the largest of the Northumbrian castles – Dunstanburgh castle.

The Anglo-Saxon 'burgh' of Dunstanburgh suggests an earlier origin than its first recorded appearance in history in the fourteenth century. The existing castle was ordered in 1313 by Thomas of Lancaster, a grandson of Henry III. It was finished in 1322 and it was not long before the Scots were attacking and being repulsed by its commander John of Gaunt, Baron of Embleton. John of Gaunt turned the Gatehouse into a massive keep, the major part of the existing ruin. When he died in 1399 the castle became the property of his son Henry of Bolingbroke who later became Henry IV of England. During the Wars of the Roses the castle was a Lancastrian stronghold changing hands several times and suffering much as a result of the fifteenth century fighting. By the middle of the sixteenth century Dunstanburgh castle was a ruin. A small harbour built on the south side of the castle once sheltered part of Henry VIII's fleet but has long since disappeared.

The harbour at unspoilt Craster, a mile and a half to the south, is used by inshore coble fishermen. It was built in 1906 by the local Craster family (resident at Craster since at least the eleventh century) for exporting the hard, local whinstone to London for kerb stones. Once tons of North Sea herring were unloaded in the harbour by the drift net fishermen for pickling and smoking. The kerb stone trade and the North Sea herring have gone but Craster's smokehouses, using imported Scottish herring, still produce kippers traditionally smoked over oak wood chips.

The six miles of the Northumbrian coast line south of Craster are rocky with only short stretches of sandy beach. There is a small beach at the tiny natural harbour of Howick Haven and from here a path leads along the coast and up along the banks of an idyllic little burn to the magnificent grounds of Howick Hall. Howick Hall was once the home of Earl Charles Grey, instigator of the 1832 Reform Act and Prime Minister of the Whig government that abolished slavery throughout the British Empire in 1833.

Continuing south the Northumbrian coastal track leads down to the sandy beach of Boulmer Haven. Boulmer is a traditional Northumbrian fishing village and anchored in the Haven, and taking the ground at low tide, are the local inshore fishermen's clinker-built cobles, open sea boats which probably evolved from the Viking longboats. Boulmer exists as a fishing community because of the protective offshore rocky reef which creates the Haven and has gaps wide enough to allow the fishermen's cobles to pass. After the Haven the shore is rocky until Seaton Point which is the north point of Alnmouth Bay.

About two miles due west and inland from Seaton Point is the little village of Lesbury and its church, like many on and near the Northumbrian coast, contains seamen's graves in the churchyard. The North Sea is a cold unforgiving sea and in an easterly gale the coast and its offshore islands have taken the lives of many seafarers. Not far away Coquet Island and the rocky banks off Seaton Point are no exception.

It is hard to believe that at one time ten coasters were owned and sailed from Alnmouth, a quiet seaside village set on a high grassy bank above the mouth of the River Aln. During the mid nineteenth century these little coasters loaded coal, grain and fertiliser to trade around the coasts of Britain and across the North Sea.

By the end of the nineteenth century the port was in decline as the river altered its course and the harbour silted up. Today the river cuts its way to the sea through the hard beach sands in an ever changing pattern of shallow trenches which are fordable at low tide, provided the river is not in flood. Walkers can travel over three miles of perfect beach to the mouth of the River Coquet at Warkworth Harbour.

The mouth of the Coquet estuary is known as Warkworth Harbour even though the large town of Amble, situated on the south bank of the river, dominates the estuary. Warkworth is situated about a mile upstream from the river mouth in a loop of the River Coquet which almost encircles the town. It was a harbour from Anglo-Saxon times until the mid nineteenth century when Amble expanded as a coal port. The river once acted as a moat for Warkworth castle which is strategically placed to guard the river crossing. King Ceolwulf of Northumbria in 737 gifted an early fortification to Lindisfarne Priory but over a hundred years later the last Northumbrian king, Osbert, took it back! The beautiful stone bridge over the Coquet at Warkworth is a good example of a fourteenth century fortified bridge and it served the town from 1379 to 1965 when the present, unattractive, bridge was built alongside. The earliest part of the existing castle was built on the site of the earlier Northumbrian castle and dates from the twelfth century. King John stayed there in 1214 and eventually Edward III sold it to the Percy family, the earls of Northumberland. When Henry of Bolingbroke became Henry IV, King of England, he owed much to the earl of Northumberland but the earl and his son, Harry Hotspur, later conspired against Bolingbroke (Henry IV) and Warkworth castle was attacked by the king's cannons. It was a ruin by the sixteenth century although the castle's keep is a well preserved example of an early fifteenth century fortification.

Busy Seahouses harbour with Bamburgh castle in the distance.

Inner Farne.

Beadnell.

Newton By The Sea: view from the Haven looking towards Dunstanburgh.

Holiday bungalows on the dunes between Newton and Embleton.

The beach near Embleton.

Embleton: the Vicar's Pele still serves as the incumbent's residence.

Dunstanburgh Castle.

Craster Harbour at low tide.

Low tide exposes rocky strata south of Cullernose Point.

Howick Hall: a late eighteenth century house built for the Grey family to the design of Newcastle architect William Newton.

Boulmer.

Cobles and waders in Boulmer Haven.

Holiday bungalow at Seaton Point.

Seaman's grave in the churchyard at Lesbury.

To the Memory of Geo:
Brown of Bedlington
Master Mariner who on
the 5th of Ap 1799 was
wreck'd on this Coast
aged 46 Years.

The Boreas blasts & Neptunes Waves
Hath tost me to and fro
In spite of both by Gods decree
I Harbour here below
Where at Anchor I do lie
With many of our Fleet
In hopes to set my Sail again
My Savour Christ to meet

Alnmouth from Church Hill. Once a busy grain port, now an unspoilt holiday resort.

Alnmouth: this view shows the original course of the Aln to a more southerly meeting with the North Sea. In 1806 a violent storm forced the river into its present channel.

Warkworth: the medieval bridge with its gatehouse.

The River Coquet at Warkworth.

The imposing Warkworth Castle.

Amble to Blyth

The River Coquet once flowed into the sea about half a mile north of the present river estuary but during a storm in 1764 it cut through the sand dunes to make its present mouth. The port of Amble owes its existence to the massive increase in demand for coal from the North East coalfields that occurred during the early part of the nineteenth century. In 1837 an Act of Parliament appointed the Warkworth Harbour Commissioners to create a coal port by building quays, straightening the river and providing berths for the colliers. By the early 1920s, 700 vessels were loading nearly three quarters of a million tons of coal per year from dozens of nearby Northumberland collieries such as Radcliffe, Broomhill and Hauxley. Incredibly, some forty years later, the colliers were gone, the pits were shut and Amble's coal trade was dead. Today Amble depends more on the fishing and tourist trade. It has always had a lively fishing community and its colourful fishing fleet of cobles and seine netters works the coast of Northumbria as well as the deeper waters of the North Sea. There has been a tradition of boatbuilding at Amble that stretches back to at least 1840 when Harrison's Boatyard was established. The yard was until recently one of the most famous for building traditional Northumberland fishing cobles. Not far from the river mouth a yacht marina has recently been built.

The lighthouse on Coquet Island a mile offshore from Amble was built in 1841 and has a similar profile to Warkworth castle. The small island is a bird sanctuary and a breeding ground for thousands of sea birds including some rare terns. Coquet Island was once a cell of Tynemouth Priory and the home of a twelfth century Danish ascetic, St Henry of Coquet or, as he is sometimes less prosaically known, Henry the Hermit.

South of Amble is Druridge Bay: six miles of curving, golden uninterrupted beach backed by steeply rising, flower filled sand dunes. Nowadays the tranquillity of Druridge Bay, often threatened by contractors digging sand and proposed nuclear power stations, is looking more assured. The open cast mines that once existed behind the dunes have been worked out and refilled and once again butterflies and kestrels hover over the dunes. The small hamlet of Druridge is situated just about in the middle of the Bay; about a mile further west is Widdrington, the turn off point for the Bay from the A1068. In the south of Druridge Bay is Cresswell, a small village with a large caravan site. The skyline in the south is dominated by the mine heads, the chimneys and the towers of the aluminium works, coal mines and power station of Lynemouth and Ellington. The beach between Cresswell and Lynemouth is black with coal dust and an example of the worst excesses of the twentieth century – uncontrolled industrial pollution.

South of this industrial desert is Newbiggin-By-The-Sea. Once a Medieval grain port, then a mining village, it is now a seaside resort with an active fishing community working a fleet of traditional Northumbrian cobles. The base of its thirteenth century church, built precariously on a rocky point, is slowly being eroded and the bones, washed out of its churchyard by the sea, are slowly being pulverised by the waves to form a coarse white sand on the shingle below.

This was a region of coal mines. The workings of the Lynemouth and Ellington collieries still extend for miles under the sea and coal seams come close to the surface of the sea bed to be washed ashore as sea coal to blacken the nearby beaches. Ashington, situated on the north bank of the River Wansbeck and some two miles inland, is one of Britain's most famous coal towns and birthplace of extraordinary footballers – the late Jackie Milburn of Newcastle United and the two brothers, Jack and Bobby Charlton.

South of Ashington is the port of Blyth which is situated on the south bank of the River Blyth. Offshore rocks protect the pier that extends almost a mile from the town of North Blyth on the north bank of the river. Not far away is an ore-carrier terminal for unloading 'bauxite', aluminium ore, which is carried by train to the aluminium smelters at Lynemouth. Upstream is the Cambois power station and the huge wooden framed coal staithes of West Staithes that used to deliver coal to the colliers from the once mighty pits of Ashington, Bedlington and Newbiggin. The wind farm on the North Blyth pier is a late-twentieth century statement on the dramatic demise of coal and an increasing public awareness of the effects of burning coal on the environment.

In the Middle Ages Blyth exported coal, salt and grain from its sheltered natural anchorage and by the end of the seventeenth century a harbour with stone quays had been constructed. At the turn of the century it was the largest coal port in Northumberland and a thriving centre of ship building and repair. The modern port was built by the Blyth Harbour and Dock Company which was created in 1854. The Blyth Harbour Commission, formed in 1882, further improved the port and the North Eastern Railway Company built large staithes for shipping out the tons of coal dug up from the once incredibly productive local pits. The South Harbour was built in 1899 and is now home to fishing boats and the cruising and racing yachts of the Royal Northumberland Yacht Club whose headquarters is an old wooden lightship.

Blyth has recently been 'modernised' but there are still some handsome buildings left: the Harbour Commission Offices, for example, that were built in 1913 and, perhaps the most visually attractive part of Blyth, Bath Terrace. This is a late eighteenth century terrace whose houses were once owned by some of Blyth's most successful shipowners. Behind the terrace is the old High Lighthouse which was built in 1788 and is said to be the oldest lighthouse in Northumbria. It was coal burning before being converted to oil, gas and finally electricity. Until 1985 the High Lighthouse was in use as a navigation beacon in conjunction with a lower light that was built nearer the harbour entrance.

Amble: neglected corner of a boatyard.

Amble: the Ocean Harvest *gets refitted and repainted ready for another season.*

Coquet Island.

Druridge Bay, from which much sand has disappeared.

Near Widdrington: the ruins of Chibburn preceptory of St John of Jerusalem.

Pele Tower at Cresswell at the southern end of Druridge Bay.

Even the Northumberland coast has its blemishes: this one between Cresswell and Lynemouth.

Newbiggin Beach.

Waste land near Newbiggin.

Woodhorn Colliery, now preserved as a museum of coal mining.

The mouth of the River Wansbeck.

Cambois Power Station and the River Blyth. The structure on the far horizon is the complex of coal staithes at North Blyth.

Wind farm on the North Blyth Pier.

Fishing from the quay in Blyth harbour. In the background a ship is unloading at the bauxite terminal.

Bath Terrace with the old navigation beacon.

Fisherman's hut in Blyth's South Harbour area.

Blyth: the piers. A morning stroller pauses to take in the light and the air.

Seaton Sluice to Whitley Bay

The safe bathing beach that lies to the south of Blyth runs into Sandy Island and the interesting little harbour of Seaton Sluice. Sandy Island is not a true island but the remains of a hill formed from dumped ship's ballast. Opposite and across the Seaton Burn is Rocky Island which was once known as 'Pans Close' after the salt pans that were used to make sea salt, a low grade salt for preserving meat and making glass, which was produced by evaporating sea water with 'small coals' that were unsuitable for export. By 1800 there were around 200 ships, colliers and bottle sloops exporting coal, salt and glass from the port.

Seaton Sluice, originally known as Hartley Pans because of the salt making, was built by Sir Ralph Delaval. It was renamed Seaton Sluice in 1690 after ingenious sluice gates were constructed to prevent the harbour from silting up. At low tide the sluice gates were closed across the Burn and horse drawn ploughs loosened the mud on the harbour bottom. When the gates were opened the disturbed silt was swept out to sea by the built up head of water. The modern road bridge over Seaton Burn marks the site of the sluice gates and their remains can be seen in the river below. In 1763 the Delavals built a bottle factory and a year later a new harbour was opened when a Cut was blasted through Rocky island. 'New Cut' was closed at each end with wooden gates that were lifted into place by cranes to create one of the first 'wet docks' in Britain. The gate slots are still evident in the west side of the Cut as are the remains of a wooden pier that was constructed on the north side of the entrance to New Cut. Despite the north pier and the New Cut, entry to the harbour was always a problem and with the development of bigger and better ports at nearby Blyth and Newcastle, Seaton Sluice declined. The last commercial ship sailed out of the harbour in 1872 with a cargo of bottles for the Channel Islands.

The Delavals owned land in the region since they came over with William the Conqueror and they were mining coal before the end of the thirteenth century. They originally developed Seaton Sluice as a coal exporting port and Admiral George Delaval built the nearby, magnificent Seaton Delaval Hall in 1729. The Hall is not far away from the infamous Hartley Pit which used to export coal from Seaton Sluice until 1862 when 204 miners died inside the pit from carbon monoxide poisoning when the beam of a pumping engine broke and the machine fell into the shaft to block forever their exit.

About halfway between Seaton Sluice and St Mary's Island, not far from Hartley, Northumbrian coal seams are exposed in the face of low sea cliffs whose tops are home to hundreds of caravans. A rock-surrounded causeway links tiny St Mary's Island with the mainland just before the seaside town of Whitley Bay.

St Mary's Island is dominated by the 126 ft high lighthouse that was built in 1898. During the excavations for its foundations, a graveyard was disturbed. The island once housed a small medieval chapel which kept a warning light burning in the sanctuary. The medieval chapel was dedicated to St Helen but the guiding lights for sailors were said to be in the hands of St Mary – hence the island's name. St Mary's Island lighthouse ceased to function in 1984 and is now part of a Visitor's Centre.

The next three miles of coast are taken up by three Northumbrian seaside resorts that have merged to form one large complex: bustling Whitley Bay, tiny Cullercoats harbour and sedate Tynemouth. There are sandy beaches, restaurants, hotels, guest houses, bed and breakfasts, flower gardens, night clubs, residential homes and all the paraphernalia of the British seaside resort. At Whitley Bay the 'Spanish City' amusement park has a building with an enormous ferro cement dome – 50 ft in diameter and six inches thick. This famous landmark was built in 1910 for Whitley Pleasure Gardens Limited.

The centrepiece of this continuous seaside development is Cullercoats. Once a tiny fishing harbour with fine stone walls and a sheltered sandy beach it has just managed, despite the amusement arcades and fish and chip shops, to hang on to its early nineteenth century elegance.

A comparatively rare easterly gale brings big breakers onto the beach at Seaton Sluice.

Seaton Sluice: the harbour.

St Mary's Island, Whitley Bay.

Spanish City, Whitley Bay.

Cullercoats Bay.

The Mouth of the Tyne

The pleasant town of Tynemouth is quieter than Whitley Bay and is blessed with a long bathing beach, Long Sands, fine eighteenth century houses, quiet residential crescents and a magnificent, ruined eleventh century priory. Long Sands stretches up to Cullercoats and for over a century has been a favourite summertime beach with the inhabitants of industrial Tyneside. Surfers come all year round, clad in thin wet suits, to ride the slowly breaking waves of the North Sea. There is a small sandy beach that lies below an imposing headland which has for centuries been the site of both a castle and a priory.

Tynemouth Priory has been much altered since it was built on the site of an Anglo Saxon monastery after the Norman Conquest. Nothing remains of the original Northumbrian monastery that once housed the remains of Oswin the king of Deira. He was buried there in 651 after being murdered in Yorkshire following his pursuit by Oswy the king of Bernicia who was trying to re-unite the kingdom of Northumbria. Tynemouth was then part of Bernicia and Oswin was buried there away from his followers in more southern Deira. The monastery was attacked several times by the Vikings and finally destroyed during a raid in 865 along with all the nuns who were sheltering inside. The Jarrow monks took over the derelict monastery in 1075. Around 1090 a Benedictine priory was built and this is the basis of the present ruins. St Henry of Coquet was buried there in 1127.

Tynemouth castle was built towards the end of the thirteenth century and at one time the outer walls enclosed the headland. Entrance to the Gatehouse was by a drawbridge and the castle, a massive and well fortified structure, played a significant role as part of the second defence line of castles in the Border Wars against the Scots.

Below the Priory, on its imposing headland and inside the impressive north wall that extends well into the sea to protect shipping entering and leaving the estuary of the River Tyne, is Prior's Haven, a tiny sand and shingle bay. Above the bay is the timbered watch house of the Tynemouth Volunteer Life Brigade which, when it was set up in 1864, was the first Volunteer Brigade in Britain.

Just upstream from Tynemouth Priory is the fishing port of North Shields. It was developed from 1225 by the monks of the monastery to replace the 'shiels' or simple huts inhabited by the local fishermen. Today the colourful in-shore trawlers and cobles that lie in its small haven are often dwarfed by the larger deep sea fishing boats that line the riverside quays across from the numerous chandlers and provisioning agents that service the local fishing industry.

Above and within the North Shields fish quay are the large white towers of two leading lights, the New High and Low lights, that are used to guide mariners through the Tyne's dangerous estuary. During Henry VIII's reign earlier high and low lights were built in 'Shelys' and had the joint role of combining defence with navigation. They were made of stone and lit by candles housed in lanterns but it was not long before the river changed its course rendering the stone lighthouses useless. Movable wooden towered lights were built in 1658 and used to navigate ships into the Tyne. They were replaced with a stone tower situated in Prior's Fort in 1672 and a second High Light was added in 1727. Candle lanterns were still used as lights. By 1805 this first pair of lights were defunct and a new pair – the New High and Low Lights – were constructed in 1808. The first Low Light became incorporated into a warehouse. The second pair of High and Low lights were lit in 1810.

Opposite Tynemouth, across the Tyne estuary, is South Shields. South Shields was once a Roman fort and storage depot, named Arbeia, that was built on a hill commanding the south bank of the River Tyne. The fort was a grain depot and garrisoned by the Fifth Cohort of Gauls but during the fourth century the Gauls were replaced by a naval force 'numerus barcarri Tigrisiensium', an elite unit of Tigris lightermen (from around Baghdad), who were more adept at ferrying stores up to the Wall forts than the Gauls.

Like North Shields, South Shields built up a thriving salt making industry and by the 1600s fishing vessels would arrive in their hundreds to load salt for preserving their catches. For centuries both North and South Shields fought with Newcastle to defend their trading rights and finally, in 1850, Newcastle was forced to relinquish some of its power over the river and its trade when parliament passed the Tyne Navigation Act. The long grey stone piers at Tynemouth and South Shields were built as part of a massive Tyne Improvement Commission scheme that deepened and transformed the lower reaches of the river and allowed ocean steamers up to Newcastle quay. Work on the north and south piers started in 1854 and, after numerous failures and breaches, they were finally completed in 1895.

There are some splendid Victorian buildings in South Shields which is now a seaside resort with good bathing beaches to the north and south of south pier which extends almost a mile into the sea. Like Tynemouth, South Shields has a Volunteer Life Brigade Watch House. This was built in 1867 and extended in 1875. Today there are only three surviving Volunteer Life Brigades left in Britain and two of them, Tynemouth and South Shields, are in their original buildings.

The crumbling limestone cliffs south of South Shields have been well sculptured by the sea. Some centuries ago Marsden Rock, 230 ft long and 140 ft high, was part of the cliff face of Marsden Bay but now, out in the bay, the rock's limestone stacks are home to myriads of sea birds. The Grotto in Marsden Bay was once the home of a miner who, in 1782, built caves into the cliff face for his family.

South of the bay is Lizard Point which has an elegant 75 ft high lighthouse. To avoid confusion with the Cornish Lizard Point lighthouse it is known as Souter Point and, when opened in 1871, was probably the first electrically illuminated lighthouse in Britain. The original carbon arc lamps were replaced by oil in 1915 only to be re-converted to electricity in 1952. South of Souter Point is the charming village of Whitburn complete with wide tree-lined streets and a duck pond.

Tynemouth: the Long Sands.

Tynemouth: the Early English east window of the ruined priory.

Tynemouth: the Life Brigade Watch House, the first building of its kind in Britain.

North Shields: the Fish Quay.

North Shields: the 'new' High Light and Low Light navigation beacons.

South Shields: the Police and Sanitary Authority Building, 1886.

South Shields: the splendidly exuberant Town Hall designed by E. E. Fetch, circa 1905.

South Shields: the Watch House on the pier.

South Shields: Marsden Rock before the archway crumbled into the sea.

Souter Point Lighthouse.

Whitburn: the village looks as if it has come from another part of Britain – Southwold on the Suffolk coast, or the Isle of Wight for instance.

From Wear to Tees

The city and port of Sunderland is situated on both sides of the mouth of the River Wear. There has been a harbour and refuge at Sunderland for at least 1,000 years but it was not until Sunderland broke Newcastle's hold on the coal trade in the Civil Wars (1642-1651), by backing parliament against staunchly royalist Newcastle, that major improvements came about and the port began to expand. In the early 1700s the Wear estuary was choked with sand, two shallow channels formed the mouth and both were difficult to navigate. In 1717 the River Wear Commissioners were formed to improve the river and port and for the next two centuries there were intensive harbourworks at Sunderland associated with the expanding coal trade and the increasingly important ship building and repair industry.

The Wear Commissioners blocked the northern channel and increased the depth and the flow of water through the southern channel by dredging. The Commissioners raised money for their activities by imposing duties on coal shipments and in 1723 they began to build a south pier to further improve the harbour. They were successful and coal exports from Sunderland doubled between 1750 and 1790. A north pier was built in 1797. Further work on the piers was carried out in the 1840s and the massive North and South Docks were built by 1850. By 1860 Sunderland's proud claim was to be 'the first ship building town in the world'.

Extensive work on the northern, Roker pier began in 1885. Huge concrete blocks faced with Aberdeen granite and some weighing over 60 tons were lifted in place before the pier was completed in 1903. The present day red and white Aberdeen granite lighthouse at the end of Roker pier was opened in 1903. Work was also started on the South pier but it was not until 1912 that the new South pier was completed. The wrought iron lighthouse built in 1856 on the end of South pier was removed to Roker sea-front when the pier was shortened in 1983.

Sunderlands dock's were fed by an extensive railway network and millions of tons of coal exported from the Durham coalfields via train and coal staithe. Today the coal trade is dead, most of the region's pits are closed and ships are no longer being built on Wearside. Sunderland has had to diversify its modern industrial base in to advanced manufacturing.

The fine pillars and solid Victorian lines of recently restored Monkwearmouth station are a testimony to the importance of the railways in the prosperity and development of Victorian Sunderland. The station was opened in 1848 and was designed by

Thomas Moore for George Hudson, the 'Railway King' who was a local MP and headed the Sunderland Dock Company that built Sunderland's South Dock in 1850. The Dock had coal staithes of the Durham and Sunderland Railway that belonged to Hudson. Today Monkwearmouth station is a railway museum and situated not far away from the beautiful St Peter's church – an important reminder that Sunderland's long history is not only industrial.

'Sundered land' might have been so named because it became separated, or 'sundered', from the ancient monastery at Monkwearmouth on the north banks of the Wear. The church of St Peter, Monkwearmouth is an ancient site of worship. Over thirteen centuries ago, in 664 Oswy, king of Northumbria, decided to link his Celtic church with Rome. A young nobleman in Oswy's court, Benedict Biscop, travelled to Rome and served in a French monastery before returning to live on the banks of the Wear at Monkwearmouth. In 674 he persuaded Oswy's son, king Ecgfrith, to grant him land where he built a church, St Peters, and a monastery. Biscop used continental craftsmen to build the stone church and French glaziers to produce the earliest English glass; forerunner of the famous glass industries of the North East and Sunderland. Bede visited the Monkwearmouth monastery and both Monkwearmouth and Jarrow monasteries developed into renowned centres of culture and learning. The Vikings attacked and destroyed much of the monastery in the eighth century. It was rebuilt as a Benedictine cell of Durham in 1083 but this was dissolved in 1536 and today little of the Northumbrian monastery remains above ground. In contrast St Peter's church is in an excellent state of repair, its western wall a statement to the skill of Biscop's stone masons.

Some two miles south of Sunderland and a little inland on a hill just north of the small port of Seaham is Seaham Hall and here in 1815 the poet Lord Byron married Anne Milbanke, daughter of Sir Ralph Milbanke. Lord Londonderry bought the Milbanke estate and developed coal mines and railway tracks. It was Lord Londonderry who built Seaham harbour in 1831 when he decided that Sunderland Docks were overcharging him for shipping coal from his Rainton pits.

There is some fine scenery south of Sunderland but the eye has to search through the debris of Britain's coal-driven industrial past. Just south of the new town of Peterlee the delightful Castle Eden Dene flows through a soft, green, wooded valley to enter the sea over a devastated, coal blackened beach. The three miles of the pretty Dene before it flows in to the sea are in stark contrast to the coal slag cliffs and soiled black beaches of the nine miles of coast that lie between Dawdon and Hartlepool. Although Durham coal field has contributed much to the economic power of modern Britain there has been a serious downside – massive industrial pollution. Millions of tons of colliery waste from the coastal pits of Dawdon, Easington, Horden and Blackhall have been dumped on the stretch of beach that lies between Dawdon and Hartlepool.

South of Blackhall Rocks the beaches become clean again and a limestone headland rises out of the sea. The headland is the home of quiet 'Old' Hartlepool. Many of the people and fishing folk of the ancient town of Old Hartlepool were not happy when it was municipally joined to neighbouring West Hartlepool, a bustling nineteenth century town complete with extensive docks and large shopping complexes, to form the town of Hartlepool.

A Northumbrian monastery, Heruteu, was built by St Aidan in Old Hartlepool. In the late twelfth/early thirteenth century the deBrus family (who came over from France with William the Conqueror) built the impressive St Hilda's abbey church on the site of St Aidan's monastery. The abbey church is named after Hilda, who was an abbess at the Northumbrian monastery, and today much of the de Brus' original building remains. The de Brus family were the ancestors of Robert Bruce, Robert I king of Scotland, and victor over the English at Bannockburn in 1314. Ironically in 1330 a wall wasbuilt round the town to keep out the Scots and its remains are evident on the south side of the headland. In medieval times Old Hartlepool was probably the most important port on the North East coast. Crusader knights sailed out of its haven.

South of Hartlepool headland and almost an extension of West Hartlepool is the quiet seaside village and pleasant sandy beach of Seaton Carew. Less pleasant, and about a mile distant is built up Seal Sands, once a sandy beach but now part of the vast petrochemical, industrial complex of Teesside. The towns of Billingham and Stockport north of the Tees and Thornaby and Middlesbrough to the south are all part of this vast complex. The largest town, Middlesbrough, was formed not so long ago in 1828 when a handful of enterprising men bought 500 acres of land and began to build a town. Enterprise, coal, iron, salt, gypsum, potash and oil did the rest.

The Tees is the southern limit of the kingdom of Northumbria that lies between the Tweed and Tees. Much has changed since Ida the Flame Bearer landed at Bamburgh.

Sunderland: these ferries were the last ships to be built on the Wear.

Monkwearmouth Station, Sunderland: designed by Thomas Moore.

Sunderland: Monkwearmouth Church, parts of which date back to the original building of 675.

Seaham Harbour, with Dawdon Colliery in the background.

Cobles and other fishing boats in the inner harbour at Seaham.

Easington Colliery, until recently a thriving mining community.

The coast near Horden.

Allotments near Blackhall.

Hartlepool: the Headland.

It is traditional in Hartlepool to weather-proof the houses as well as the boats.

Seaton Carew: sandy beach and art deco seaside architecture.

Newport Bridge across the River Tees.